The MANTRA *of* JABEZ

Upturned Table Parody Series

CANON PRESS • MOSCOW, IDAHO

The
MANTRA

Break on Through to the Other Side

of JABEZ

DOUGLAS M. JONES
WITH DOUGLAS M. JONES

Douglas M. Jones III, *The Mantra of Jabez*

© 2001 by Douglas M. Jones III

Published by Canon Press
P.O. Box 8729, Moscow, ID 83843
800–488–2034 / www.canonpress.org

05 04 03 02 01   9 8 7 6 5 4 3 2 1

Cover mimicry by Paige Atwood
Cover Image: The Evangelical Okey-Dokey

Scripture quotations in this publication are taken from the *Holy Bible: King James Version.*

ISBN: 1-885767-88-9

TABLE OF CONTENTS

PREFACE

Dear Newbie,

I want to teach you how to chant a daring mantra that, unlike burdensome traditional prayers, God always has to answer. It is brief, which is really nifty for modern evangelical attention spans—only one sentence with four parts. You can even shorten it more if you remove all the consonants. Just hum the vowels. It's tucked away in a silly part of the Bible, but I believe it contains an automatic formula for favor with God.

This mantra has radically changed what I expect from God and what I experience every day by His power. In fact, thousands of believers who are humming it are seeing wonderfully short-term things happen on a regular basis. Many of them are even touching fewer and fewer material things!

Will you join me for a personal exploration of the mantra of Jabez? Anyone can hop on. It doesn't demand anything of you, just mouthing some words.

1

LITTLE MANTRA, GIANT SCORE

Jabez called on the God of Israel

The little book you're holding is about what happens when bored, sentimental Evangelicals decide to reach for a whiz-bang life, like that on MTV—flash, flash, flash—which, as it turns out, is exactly the kind God promises.

My own story starts in a kitchen with yellow counters, rectangular drawer fronts, a white refrigerator, AC electricity, and Texas-sized raindrops pelting transparent windows. It was my senior year at one of those liberating seminaries that teach you to minister quickly and to delight in short-term thinking because we have no future on earth.

I was thinking about what would come next. Where would I throw my training? As I stood there in that yellow-countered kitchen with the rectangular drawer fronts, I thought of the challenge I'd heard from the seminary chaplain earlier that week. "Want a bigger vision for your life?" he had asked. "Then sign up to be a *kipper* for God." A kipper, as the chaplain explained it, was a small fish, smoked and salted, that is kept in a dark, vacuum-sealed tin. He took as his text the briefest of Bible biographies: "And Jabez was more honorable than his brethren" (1 Chronicles 4:9). It turns out that Jabez wanted to be a kipper for God, a man vacuum-preserved from outside temptations who was instantly ready to be eaten but not satisfying anyone's hunger. End of verse. End of Bible story.

A kipper is not to be confused with a gipper. "Win one for the kipper" would have produced an entirely different president.

Lord, I think I want to be a kipper for you, I prayed as I looked out that square window with those Texas-sized raindrops smacking and smacking it.

But I was puzzled. *What exactly did Jabez do to rise above the rest?* Sure the text says that he was more *honorable* than his brothers, but that can't be it. Examining that would require me to think about covenants and Mosaic law and all those nasty commandments that

David goes on so long about in Psalm 119. It can't be based on Jabez's virtue; that sounds like works-righteousness. Yick.

Something in the words of the prayer itself had to explain the mystery. It had to. Of course, somewhere it says that "the effectual fervent prayer of a *righteous* man avails much," but think of the long, boring time involved in cultivating biblical virtues like righteousness. We're saved by faith alone after all, and that's quick like a Dodge commercial. The rapture may happen any moment too. An easier evangelical answer must be found.

I bent over my Bible, and reading the prayer over and over and over and over, I searched with all my individualistic heart for the future God had for modern people who didn't have decades to cultivate honor.

The next morning, I chanted Jabez's mantra word for word.

And the next.

And the next.

And a gobb more nexts.

Thirty years later, I haven't stopped. Though I affirm to you that I've never chanted it on a street corner.

In the pages of this little book (whose price the publisher has conveniently set at $9.99, really not at all $10.00, but the more direct and forthright $9.99), I want to introduce you to the amazing truths of Jabez's mantra and prepare you to turn the faucet of God's blessing just like that <finger-snapping sound>.

Just ask the man who had no future.

THE PRODIGY OF A BORING LIST

Someone once said that there is really very little difference between differing people—but that little difference is the same difference. I have no idea what that means either, but it reminds me of Jabez.

You can think of him as the Prodigy of Genealogy or the Bible's Little Big Man or God's Quiet Kipper or Hoss on *Bonanza*. You'll find him in one of the most boring sections of the Bible, you know, all those yammer-yammer-yammer genealogies of Hebrew names that mean nothing and are hard to get your lips around. Talk about boring! Boy, I don't know what God was thinking here. *Perez, Hezron, and Carmi, and Hur, and Shobal. . . .* I'd certainly forgive you if you suddenly considered putting this book aside and reaching for your TV remote—flash, flash, flash.

In the midst of all this meaningless genealogical covenantal history and antithesis stuff, a real story that even modern Evangelicals can understand breaks through.

> And Jabez was more honorable than his brethren: and his mother called his name Jabez, saying, because I bore him with sorrow. And Jabez called on the God of Israel, saying, "Oh that You would bless me indeed, and enlarge my coast, and that Your hand might be with me, and that You would keep me from evil, that it may not grieve me!" And God granted him that which he requested. (1 Chronicles 4:9–10)

It's as if the historian stops in middrone to highlight Jabez. But what was the *secret* to the enduring reputation of Jabez? You can Skim-Thru-the-Bible from front to back, as I have taught millions to do, and you won't find any more info about Jabez than in this prayer, assuming we're still agreeing to set aside that "honor" thingy:

- Things started badly for an unknown guy.
- He chanted an unusual, one sentence mantra.
- Great things happened automatically.

Clearly, then, by good and necessary seminary inference, the great outcome can be traced to Jabez's little mantra. Obviously something about these little letters and symbols changed Jabez's life and left a permanent mark on the history books of Israel. Here is that prayer nicely centered for you:

> Oh that You would bless me indeed,
>   and enlarge my territory,
>   and that Your hand might be with me,
>   and that You would keep me from evil.

These mantra markings may look unremarkable, but just under the surface of each lies a really giant paradigm breaker. Remember those words, *paradigm breaker*. Keep saying them over and over, because though you may read the exposition of each line in the following chapters and think, "jeepers, that's painfully trivial after thirty years of meditating on those verses," remember to keep saying, *paradigm breaker, paradigm breaker, paradigm breaker.*

In the pages to come, I want to show you just how dramatically each of Jabez's requests can automatically release something miraculous in your life, no matter how shallow and immature your walk is, or even if you watch too much TV, are petty with your spouse, send your kids to public schools, and think *Left Behind* is brilliant literature.

Remember to keep saying, paradigm breaker *but be careful not to pronounce the "g" or else you'll make some people giggle in their palms.*

LIVING BEYOND CHASTISEMENT

What I have to share with you has been opening up God's mighty work for many years. Recently, I was in Dallas to teach on the Jabez blessing to an audience of 9,000. Did you see that number? That's like, I dunno, a Mormon sorta number. Anyway, over lunch, a man said to me, "I've been chanting the Jabez mantra for ten years." Across the table, a friend said he'd been chanting it for fifteen years. Another said twenty years. I told them, "Friends, I've been chanting Jabez for more than *half my life!*" Note that exclamation mark. "But I swear I've never done it on a street corner." A nasty little shouting match started up, and then it quickly turned to wrestling, and, of course, we scattered all of our jello all over the floor. By the end we were all shouting the mantra at each other.

The purpose of these little side quotes is to provide a summary for those who struggle with reading a whole booklet.

But the point is that because you're reading this booklet, I believe you share my desire for a more whiz-bang life without pain. When you stand before God to give your final accounting, you want to hear "~~You just didn't get it, did you?~~" I mean, "Well done."

Think of it this way: instead of begging for a cup of water near the river's edge, you chant the little mantra with the giant score and get pulled under by the current. Or, maybe, you jump in but just skim along the surface for a very long time. Yeah, that's it. That's what God wants.

2

So Why Not Twist It?

Oh, that You would bless me indeed!

Y ou're at one of those cheesy spiritual retreats in the mountains with others who want to hear trite and sentimental chats about how important your needs and feelings are in the whole history of Christendom. You will certainly be a new person for three or four days afterwards. You have been matched with a seventy-year-old mentor, and he's been touching lives longer than you've been around.

On the way to the showers, whose spray doesn't remind you of those Texas-sized rain drops I mentioned earlier, you nosily peep through his ajar door and hear him praying. You can't resist. *How exactly does a giant of the faith begin his prayers?*

The really amazing thing is that this fictional mentor starts praying in just the manner that this booklet teaches! How remarkable! Startled by this discovery on the way to your shower, you suddenly realize that this mentor is truly a *kipper* for God. He hasn't matured at all in seventy years.

First of all, you suspect he heard you breathing at his door, so he prayed aloud so you could hear him and show off. Second, you despair because this seventy-year-old should have long ago been exasperated by the shallowness of these evangelical retreats and denounced them. You worry, "Will I be as immature and foolish when I'm that age?" Will I be a kipper for God who still has no clue about the social implications of the Trinity or the riches of covenant succession in family life or the power of the Incarnation for fighting hidden pietisms or finding the miraculous in the ordinary parts of creation or learning the riches of aesthetic living from Ecclesiastes? Will I be that pathetic? Probably. But at least chanting Jabez's mantra will give you a little buzz. The sincerity alone will make you feel significant.

The capital of Texas is Austin, named after Steve Austin, the bionic man.

NOT PAIN, BUT GAIN

First, let's take a more in-depth look at Jabez's history. The problem, as noted earlier, is that we have only about sixteen words concerning him in Scripture itself, so I'll just go ahead and make some stuff up, otherwise, this booklet would be just an editorial.

As far as we can tell, Jabez lived in southern Israel after the conquest of Canaan, a little toward the left edge of town near the cattle depot. Yet his story really begins with his name: "His mother called his name Jabez, saying, 'Because I bore him in pain.'" In Hebrew, the word *Jabez* means "pain" or "excruciating pain" or "painful pain." A literal rendering, which is the only path to truth, mighta-could read, "This boy is a pain in the neck, and I will make sure his friends make fun of him." Mom was quite a card. Only God knows for sure what caused her pain, but I know the boy was teased incessantly through his teenage years.

Finally Jabez gets fed up and bursts out in this mantra of his: "Oh, that you would bless me *indeed*." The Hebrew for *indeed* is like five exclamation marks, like this—!!!!! This proves how serious he was.

From our little text alone, I can picture Jabez standing before a massive gray, rectangular gate, recessed in about eleven and a half feet into a sky-high wall. Weighed down by the sorrow of his past, the incessant teasing, the dreariness of his present, and his constant whining, he sees only impossibility, i.e., that big gate in his way. But raising his hands, he starts to chant the mantra and automatically the walls crumble down on top of him. No, sorry, he skims over the top, no that was that river thing. The gates open wide, and he sees a field of blessings stretching to the horizon.

And all he had to do was chant his words. No curses. No chastisements. No wisdom. No virtue. Just use the mantra to twist the faucet, and it all comes flowing out. You might be a whiner or a jerk or clueless, but the mantra opens faucets of blessings. And God can't stop it.

Notice that Jabez leaves the nature of the blessings entirely up to God. This kind of radical trust has nothing at all, really and truly, to do with the common name-it-and-claim-it nonsense. No. Those folks are obsessed about nasty material things. Jabez's mantra is about spiritual things only. After all, why get stuff the antichrist will take?

MR. YOU GOES TO HEAVEN

Imagine that heaven is a trivial, bureaucratic place much like the place in all those jokes where Peter wears wings and stands at the gate. Then imagine that heaven is really focused on you as the goal, not on extending the kingdom throughout the earth and glorifying God. Your feelings and needs are what it's all about. Then imagine that, say, a Mr. You goes to heaven, and winged-Peter shows him around like a tourguide at Disneyland. Peter refuses to show Mr. You one particular building Mr. You really, really wants to see, and after Mr. You's constant complaining, Peter finally relents.

Inside the building are shelves full of little boxes with names on them in alphabetical order in English. Mr. You rushes down aisle after aisle, tracking the alphabet all the way to the Y's. Peter keeps pace behind him, but he's breathing hard. Mr. You rips the red ribbon and duct tape off his box and stares inside, while Peter cleans up after him.

There in the box are all the blessings that God wanted to give Mr. You while on earth, but Mr. You failed to ask for. Even though there's no limit to God's goodness, if you don't ask for a blessing, God won't give it.

Suddenly, Mr. You turns on Peter, who is standing there wide-eyed, hands full of ribbon and duct tape.

"I don't mind," says Mr. You, "missing all these blessings on earth, since I'm here now, and I had a good time down there, but—"

"Yeah?" says Peter.

In the original book Mr. You was played by a Mr. Jones, but that hit too close to home.

"But doesn't it bother you that God keeps all these blessings card-catalogued just to spite us when we get here?"

Peter frowns. "Well. . . uh. . . I don't think—"

Mr. You interjects, "That seems pretty small and petty doesn't it? Is God motivated by resentment like us?"

Peter grabs Mr. You's lapel, "Look, he didn't catalogue all this by himself. He had help."

"Oh," says Mr. You.

"Anyway," Peter says, "this illustration is supposed to explain how the Jabez mantra works. Let's keep to that."

"Okay," says Mr. You, staring at his feet.

Through this simple, formulaic mantra, you can change your future. You can change what happens one minute from now, one second from now, before you reach the end of this sentence. There. Just twist the faucet.

3

Living Extra Large for God

Oh, that you would enlarge my territory!

The next part of the Jabez mantra—a plea for more territory—is where you make some sounds not for more territory as the text says but for more ethereal opportunities to put sentences into other people's heads. That's really what ministry is, isn't it—getting sentences into peoples heads?

It would be all too easy to read this text for what it says, but to ask for more land is a bit too earthy and dirty. After all, the Tribulation is coming; real land isn't important. And Jabez was in the dark ages of the Old Testament where God overlooked their silly obsessions.

For us, it's easier to read *territory* not as land but as opportunity. After all, *territory* has the word *terr* or *tear* in it, and if you tear something, then you have at least two opportunities to make other stuff.

No matter what your vocation, then, the highest form

of Jabez's mantra for more territory might sound something like this:

> *O God and King, please expand my opportunities and my impact in such a way that I can help insert sentences into other people's heads.*

When you pray like this, you'll start to breathe hard.

NOT LITERAL BOUNDARY LINES

During a weeklong speaking engagement some years ago at a large Christian college in California, I challenged the students to say the Jabez mantra for more "territory." I suggested that the 2000-member college set a ministry goal far beyond their wildest expectations.

Though the word "gnosticism" doesn't appear in the body of this parody, it should. Oh look, here it is again: "gnosticism."

"Why not look at the globe and pick an island like Trinidad?" I suggested. "Put together a team of students, get a DC–10, then take over the island for God."

Some students roared. Some questioned my sanity.

Others thought my suggestion didn't match my own talk.

"Why do we have to take a puny island? Why can't we take Los Angeles?" The crowd roared its support.

Their chanting for L.A. filled the auditorium. I shuffled my papers a bit and looked at my watch.

"Well," I said. "You've got to start small."

Boos filled my ears. I waved my hands for silence. I buckled under pressure. They were right.

"Okay, okay, go take L.A., you crazy kids!" I said. Wall-shaking shouts and applause came back. I smiled.

One young lady stood up and shouted, "First, we'll take over all the L.A. welfare systems and hospices and hospitals, then be creative in all the L.A. arts, then help single mothers nurture their children, then inspire a new Christian architecture and literature, then reform the prisons according to biblical principle, then help—"

"Whoa sister!" I shouted. "When Jabez and I say *territory* we don't mean all this earthy stuff. I'm just talking about opportunity to get sentences into people's heads. That's what the mantra is all about—sentences. All this other stuff is going to be *left behind*."

"Oh, yeah," she said and sat down.

After I returned home, the college was swept by a vision for "territory" over the subsequent months. They had mounted a major mission project called Operation Sentences into Their Heads. Their objective: assemble a team of student workers, charter a jet, and—you guessed it—fly to the island of Trinidad for a summer of putting sentences into people's heads.

That is exactly what they did. The college president called Operation Sentences into Their Heads the single most significant student ministry in the college's history. The beautiful part is that it all came from saying a mantra. It required no long term hopes, cultivated virtues, or maturity. Just whiz-bang, get the sentences out there. And they didn't even have to worry about Trinidad actually maturing as a Christian culture.

The island of Trinidad lies between 10° 2' and 11°12' N. Latitude, and 60°30' and 61°56' W. Longitude. The average length of Trinidad is 80 km and its average breadth is 59 km. A quiz will follow.

Everything there is the same as ever. But the sentences got declared that summer. That's ministry.

MORE SENTENCE APPOINTMENTS

The Jabez mantra is a revolutionary request. It is rare to hear anyone plead, "God please give me more opportunity to say some Christian sentences." But right away you'll sense the pleasure God feels in your request and His urgency to get out more sentences through you. People will show up on your doorstep or at a table next to you. They're just waiting for Christian sentences. I call these Jabez appointments.

I remember asking for one when I was aboard a ship off the coast of Turkey. When it docked, instead of taking the tour, I wandered around saying the mantra, begging for an opportunity to pass on some Christian sentences—*Enlarge my territory*. A few minutes later, a young American living there approached me and said his wife was leaving him.

"Want a few sentences?" I said. He did.

When you start asking in earnest—begging—for more sentence appointments, God will bring them. You'll be

like Peter and John who were instantly given great wisdom and virtue without any time lags. Of course, even if
you run away from opportunities, God might force you
to them, like Jonah or Moses, but those are sorta reverse
mantra things that don't really fit. It's like the faucet could
turn on by itself or something. Anyway, to pray for larger
borders is to ask for miracles.

The most exhilarating miracles in my life have
always started with a bold request to expand the opportunity for giving out Christian sentences *a lot,* an over-
whelmingly big vision–like a dinky island for a summer.
Big steps like that need God. I've seen it happen hun-
dreds of time. You too can have a front row seat in a life
of sentence appointments. Just chant the mantra, and
the world will soon be full of Christian sentences, ever
floating into intellects, but never coming down to earth.
That's excitement.

4

Touched by
Immaturity

Oh, that Your hand would be with me!

Now you've done it. You're overwhelmed by all the responsibilities that come along with sentence giving. You are unable to hold onto the life you chanted for.

When believers start chanting the mantra of territory, they quickly find themselves in this kind of unexpected quandary; they often feel afraid. Misled. Abandoned. Teed off. Weepy.

Of course, every Christian ought to live the truth that every aspect of our life is dependent upon the grace of God. The universe doesn't run by cause and effect. It runs by the mysteries of grace, and God is Lord, not ourselves. God uses the broken and humble to show forth His power. But I'm after something much more thrilling—*perpetual immaturity*. Now that may sound bad, but which is more exciting: being a mature grown-up

30

who has to take responsibility for judgments and wisdom or being a child who gets to lay back and never learn wisdom? Of course, it's better to be a kid. After all, Jesus did say that we have to be little children.

Jabez's mantra itself shows us this. I can see through the words of the mantra itself that Jabez ran into trouble. He had prayed for an enlarged territory, God gave it to him, and it was too much. So like a child he quickly added the next part of the prayer, "Oh, that Your hand would be with me." Jabez knew he needed a divine hand—and fast. Almost all spiritual things should happen fast, thirty days max. But again, this isn't that basic dependence that all Christians should live; it's that especially immature dependence that God likes where we can just lean back, shut our eyes, and not worry about the consequences. As Jesus Himself said somewhere, "When you intend to build a tower, don't sit down first and count the cost, whether you have enough to finish it. Just go ahead and

Perpetual motion isn't possible, but perpetual immaturity can go on forever, even decades.

let them say, this man began to build and was not able to finish it." That's real dependence.

LADDER TO THE SKY

One day when our kids were preschoolers, my wife and I found ourselves in a large city park, the sort that makes a grown man want to skip and squeal and pull pigtails. The most enticing parts were the three slides, not one but three—small, medium, and giant. My son ran immediately for the smallest slide, and I got a little edgy.

"Should I go with him?"

"Ease up, cowboy," said my wife.

Then he moved to the medium slide. He got halfway up and looked at Mom who ignored him.

"Honey, I ought to help him out," I said.

"I don't want a wimp for a son," she said. "Let him tough it out."

He slid down just fine. I breathed easier. But then he ran for the giant slide.

"I don't think he should do that by himself," I said.

My wife sighed. "Do you really want a son neutered by safety all his life?"

"No I, I, I . . . guess not," I said.

"Then let me handle this," she said, as my son stopped halfway up the ladder and called out to me.

My wife cupped her hands and shouted at him, "You gird up your loins, boy, and get to the top right now! Move, move, move!" He began to wimper like a pinned weasel. So did the boy.

In a flash, I peeled off my wife's grip from my wrist and climbed up after boy-boy. We got to the top, and I wrapped my arms around him as we squealed down the slide together. Sure my wife was right, and I probably scarred him for life, but it was important for this chapter.

She was about to yell at our son, "Go fast! Take chances!" But if everyone did that where would evangelical children learn to be so annoyingly sentimental?

My coddling of my son is the way God likes to keep us perpetually immature too. It's not just creaturely dependence. It's total immaturity: *God carried me, gave me the words, gave me the power–and it is wonderful immaturity.* It's like praying, "Give us this day our daily bread," and then not having to get a job! Wow.

It's like Abraham going up to sacrifice Isaac. I'm sure all the way up, God was encouraging Abraham not to worry, all the time wrapping His arms around panicky Abraham. Similarly, the Father must have been coddling His own Son warmly, when Jesus cried out, "Why have You forsaken Me?"

God longs to coddle us as babies all our lives. How else could he tell us, "You have need of milk, not strong meat"? (Heb. 5:12)

The key to having confidence amidst your perpetual immaturity is a special surge of feeling in your muscles that is always the Holy Spirit. Oddly, I have even heard that some mature Christians have never felt this. That's really the only way to know that God is with you. When Jesus sent the Holy Spirit, He touched these ordinary believers with a powerful surge of immaturity. They didn't have to do squat or be squat. They just lay there, and poof like magic, they were ready. In fact, you'll notice in Luke's account that the phrase "filled with the Spirit" is often linked to its consequence: They "spoke with boldness." That adrenaline-like surge *through them* was always the Holy Spirit. That is why Scripture says, "faith is that surge feeling in things hoped for, the adrenaline rush of things not seen" (Heb. 11:1). Chanting the mantra opens the faucet for the same surge. Just say the words.

MANTRA AND A MAGIC SHOW

I saw how this power of perpetual immaturity worked one summer in suburban Long Island, New York, United States of America. I was serving as a youth pastor for twelve high school students. Our objective: to put Christian sentences in the heads of the neighborhood youth within six weeks. All of us felt overwhelmed, but we used the Jabez mantra to get our backyards overflowing with over one hundred kids in Bible studies. So many sentences were flowing into their heads we were giddy.

Harry Houdini was so versatile with his toes that he could use them to pick locks and feed himself from a nicely set table. But not at the same time.

Out at the beach, the Jabez mantra was answered quite appropriately by means of some magic tricks I learned. We unrolled our free magic show there in the beach in front of over a hundred folks. Then we'd bait and switch. We would start inserting Christian sentences in their heads, explaining that magic and the gospel had a lot in common. Just chant the mantra and miraculous things automatically happen. It sorta like Harry Potter: the formulas work regardless of the maturity or virtue of the chanter. Pretty neat.

By the end of summer, 1200 people had Christian sentences inserted in their heads. And our twelve kids went home convinced that God can get sentences into any head. All this because we chanted the mantra.

Like any loving dad at the playground, God is watching and waiting to coddle you so that you don't have to grow up. You and I are only one mantra away from inexplicable, surging exploits. Ask every day for the Father's coddle and soon you'll be basking in immaturity.

5

KEEPING VACUUM SEALED

Oh, that you would keep me from evil!

After the Jabez mantra opens the faucet for supernatural immaturity, you can't expect to be strong enough to be able to withstand temptation. Can babes withstand candy? Of course not. So the mantra of Jabez seeks to remove us completely from the world of sin. Why play anywhere near Satan? He always makes us come in second. And since we don't have time to develop spiritual habits and virtues, we can never resist the devil. Being vacuum sealed is part of being a baby kipper.

PERILS OF SUCCESS

It is a law of nature that God always curses success. He must hate it, even when He does it. Success always stems from arrogance and pride, and so it has to fall. That's why we can't hope that the Great Commission will really and truly succeed. Personal sanctification is a bit of a fraud too. If the Holy Spirit were really able to mature people out of childish lusts, then why do so many ministers fall into sin, drop out of ministry, and leave a mess in their wake? It's quite unbelievable, especially given the number of Christian sentences in their heads. But it does show us that real maturity isn't possible. The Holy Spirit doesn't work that way, so it's best just to become vacuum-sealed as quickly as possible.

When booklets like this talk about temptation, we always mean sexual temptation, nothing else. One of the grand benefits of holding to a very literalistic, scientific, nonpoetic, nonsymbolic grid of biblical interpretation is that it allows one always to be eternally threatened by sexual temptation of the silliest sort. Pornography looks at sex from a scientific angle; their bodies are just measurable quantities without personality or history or community. You can capture all of their facts with formulas, and we observers keep a nice laboratory distance from the objects in view. The literalist elite use the same vision everywhere; we look at our Bibles literally/scientifically, as well as our sexuality—wife and porn are examined through the same sort of microscope. This helps keep us in the thrill of perpetual immaturity.

The dangerous thing would be to look at the world poetically or symbolically. That always leads to liberalism, communism, and sonnets. If we were to look at the world poetically, then porn would too quickly lose its appeal. A poetic vision allows me to see goodness and beauty far beyond what the microscope could pick up. But porn stars are impersonal, disconnected from my marriage history and my wife's sacrifices for goodness. In the poetic vision, the older my wife gets the more lovely and alluring she becomes because her history, sacrifice, and goodness cannot be separated from her body. Everyone would pale beside her maturing poetry.

Now don't go start talkin' 'bout no poetry with all them fancy dancy words and stuff. Strip all that stuff away for truth, like them Locke and Aristotle said.

At some point, this could get so dangerous that porn would actually look ugly, because it tries to strip goodness from beauty. In this vision, we would have to worry that forty-year-old men would no longer find teen-age girls sexually alluring because their bodies are sym-bolically tied to youthful shallowness and silliness. But thank goodness for literality in our walk. We don't have to worry about any of this. We can just flee at the faint-est hint of a breast in our vicinity.

Years ago I had completed a week of special meet-ings in Chicago in the middle of the country. I was so exhausted that as I sat in the airplane headed home, I pleaded, "O Lord, I have no resistance left. I am com-pletely worn out in Your service. I can't handle tempta-tion now. Please keep me vacuum sealed from evil."

But I was seated in a middle seat, and as the plane took off, the two men on either side of me whipped out porn magazines or maybe they were Legos? I can't re-member. I cried out under my breath, "Lord, I thought we had a deal here," and groaned in my spirit to be vacuum sealed. I had such an attraction to those toys that I could barely keep my hands off them. I too wanted to snap those color blocks together bit by bit and giggle at my creation. Yet the men on either side kept spinning the vivid rectangles into amazing spectacles. I closed my eyes so tightly I saw shadows behind shadows. I wouldn't be able to stand it much more. Then all of a sudden, God made those men put away their Legos. They simultaneously packed them up and slid the porn magazines into their brief cases. I mean Legos— they slid the Legos away.

God had preserved me in simple literality—beauty and goodness were sundered completely. But it goes to show you that men can never outgrow Legos or teenagers. Our natural bodily instincts will always be tempted to sin, no matter how sanctified. Neither maturity nor Holy Spirit can overcome the lure of those little blocks: "when I became a man, I couldn't get away from childish things" (1 Corinthians 13:11ish). That's why it's important to drop all our weapons of resistance. There is no use against such temptation. The literal leaves us nicely open to live

The LEGO Company founder Ole Kirk Christiansen invented the term LEGO in 1932. Born out of the two Danish words "LEg GOdt" meaning "play well" in English and "better than TV" in Swahili.

only on the surface of life, simplistically open to the devil's shots. That's why we desperately need books like this.

PLAYING KEEP AWAY

Being vacuum sealed is so crucial because Satan is more omniscient than God. He's much faster too. He can boogie his little body around to every individual evangelical and ruin his or her day. Nothing is more important for him than stopping the attack of those who are perpetually immature. What could be more dangerous to his kingdom than a legion of whining Christians?

That's the main reason why we must always flee evil as the Jabez mantra says. Yet somehow we don't even think to ask God simply to keep us away from temptation and keep that busy devil at bay in our daily lives. But Jesus Himself taught us to pray, "And lead us not into temptation, but deliver us from evil" (Matthew 6:13). There's nothing in that verse about maturity or spiritual habits to resist. Not a word about confrontation. Come to think of it, "give us this day our daily bread" doesn't say anything at all about paychecks either. So those are out. Hey, and "forgive us our debts" doesn't mention Christ's atonement, so maybe . . . but I digress.

Still the point is that God longs to hear you plead to flee evil. Jabez would tell us, "Stay out of the arena of temptation whenever possible, but never live in fear or defeat, but not exactly success either since that will fail, just hover somewhere in between." Do you really believe that God can keep you from evil? He has done it for millions of people who chant the Jabez mantra.

If elephants and lions were transparent, then they could be better protected from poachers. But mating might be problematic.

At first, God would keep porn magazines out of my line of sight. I once walked by a newstand and just then a large man knocked me over. When I got up the magazines had vanished. Then my friends and I chanted the mantra more, our eyes developed those floating black boxes like on those TV police shows. We simply couldn't see naked things at all. Then banks started disappearing in my town when I lost my temper from trying to balance my check book. Then my friends and family started dying off, and soon I never faced interpersonal squabbles anymore. My car engine soon vanished, too, as did my bad teeth. Soon my aging body became transparent. I couldn't believe it at first. As I write this sentence, my see-through fingers float pristinely just above the keys, and my butt doesn't touch the evil fabric in my chair. Step by step God removed every temptation from my life. It is true liberation.

Ask the thousands who have been freed from temptation by chanting the mantra. Do you trust God to make every material thing invisible? Your vision may be too small. Don't accept half measures or mediocre expectations; don't box God in. He Himself taught us to ask to be kept from evil. Don't keep yourself from being vacuum sealed.

6

WELCOME TO THE BUNGEE-JUMP

Jabez was more honorable than his brothers.

Hopefully we are far enough away from the opening text about Jabez that you won't notice an important switch. Given the vast information we have about Jabez and his mantra, it's clear now that Jabez's mantra *earned* him a "more honorable" award from God. Now the text actually reverses the chronological order and appears to say that Jabez was honorable and *then* God answered his prayer, but that really undoes my whole instant Christianity assumption. And anyway, shouldn't we better view this verse's chronology through Tim LaHaye spectacles, where "quickly" means wait for two thousand years, and past events are forced into the future? From that angle, Jabez's mantra made him honorable. Phew.

Because of the magic of the mantra you too can have a life of constant exhilaration, a life of constant miracles like the surging thrill of a bungee jump—you know, where frat boys wrap King-Kong rubber bands around their ankles and jump off pinnacles. Now imagine doing that all day long, zing-whiz, zing-whiz, zing-whiz: that's what the Christian life should be.

GOD'S BUNGEE BOUNCING ME NOW

I think the immediacy—the "now-ness"—of serving God is one of the most exciting aspects of living for God's Bungee jump. If you chant the mantra, you will start to thrive in the present to a degree most Christians have never thought possible.

Think about it: How would your day unfold if you believed that God wants to create sentence-insertion opportunities with every person you meet, all while you have the confidence that God's powerful hand is directing you every moment you minister?

Hopefully you noticed that last word *minister*. That's the key to a great Bungee-Christian life. You have to realize that real ministry is full-time work, full-time evangelism, counseling, and sentence insertion. That's where the bungee thrill comes in. It's only in real ministry that you can do all the exciting things I'm talking about—cruising by Turkey, lecturing in Chicago, doing magic on Long Island, talking to divorcees in airports, setting up international ministries. That's the sort of thing that counts as ministry. God can't really be happy with your life unless you're a full-time pastor or teacher.

But Jabez's mantra isn't just for those in genuinely holy callings. So you will need to change. If you're stuck in the house all day doing laundry, prepping meals, and wiping kids or at the office shuffling employees or filling out forms, you need to plan ahead more. Get all those less holy things done much

Do not try this at home. If you have a problem with porn, please don't aim to evangelize utter babes. Skip one for the kipper.

earlier in day, so you can get out on the street quicker so God can expand you. As James exhorts us, "Many of you should become teachers, knowing that that's the only calling God truly likes" (James 3:1).

During the past five years, I've been putting the mantra to a very specific test with astounding results. I hum the mantra, asking God for more real ministry, then following the nudge of the Holy Spirit, I ask a complete stranger, "How can I help you?" Many of them correct my grammar, but others just say, "Beat it creepo." But once at the Atlanta airport, in transit between real holy ministry events, I walked up to a stunning divorcee businesswoman, wearing all sorts of expensive Italian accessories. I blurted out, "What can I do for you?"

"Beat it creepo," she said.

"No really, what can I do for you?" I said.

"I'm going to call security if you don't leave me alone," she said sideways.

"No really, what can I do for you?" I said again.

"Oh, you must be one of those guys with the Jabez mantra," she said. "Six others beat you already." She paused. "Here's what you can do then," she said. My eyes lit up—it was one of those Christian sentence moments, I could tell.

She looked directly at me and said, "Be human! You're too ethereal and ghostly. You're fingers aren't even touching your briefcase, for Pete's sake," she said. "Grow up. Doesn't the Incarnation mean anything? Life is more than passing out Christian sentences. Pure religion is to visit the fatherless and widows in their affliction. Show me how to see the glory of God in the ordinary things of life; show me how to be faithful and find meaning in the quotidian; show me how to 'eat my bread with joy and drink my wine with a merry heart' like Solomon says. Show me how to raise children so that, from them, generations will rise up and count me blessed. Show me how to live life artfully. Show me . . . ."

"Quotidian" is fun to say. I wish I could say it all day. I'll say it in the garden and say it in the field, hay, hay, hay hay, hay.

She kept shouting after me as I wandered off. There was no helping her. She just didn't get it. Not only did all those things require time and maturity and a future (and wine!), but they didn't involve real ministry. They would require seeing the world and life poetically, as if the heavens declared the glory of God or "day unto day uttered speech." But God isn't concerned with the little things: "He that is faithful in the big things of ministerial work, he shall be blessed" (Luke 16:10).

Housewives and office workers and engineers and children can't really live the Christian life. They are too encumbered by earthy things. They actually touch stuff with their fingers. An exciting life means that you find exhilaration in big, daily miracles. If we spent our time, seeing the miraculous in ordinary things—in labor and cleaning and raising children and creating, then God would have no means by which to get out His sentences. If ordinary Christians were truly able to delight in the divine poetry of housework, flowers, clothes, oceans, car repair, and plumbing, if they were able to see the utter glory of God in every mundane thing, then who would buy this booklet? Who would think that ministry only equals evangelistic service? No one would want my bungee mantra.

THE CIRCLE OF BUNGEES

Thank goodness no one believes that stuff anymore. But as you continue chanting the Jabez mantra bungee things will happen to you. I promise you that you will see a direct link because you prayed after the following pattern:

• Ask God to make you a real full-time pastor-evangelist every day. Meditate on the bumper stickers: "If God is your co-pilot: Switch seats" or "We're too blessed to be depressed."

• Plead for more opportunities to do the only important work of sentence input. Meditate on the bumper stickers: "Friends don't let friends go to hell" or "For all you do, His blood's for you!"

• Feel the surge of adrenaline and call this the Holy Spirit no matter what foolishness you say. Meditate on the bumper sticker: "Let go and let God."

• Ask God to keep you vacuum sealed and try not to pee much. Think of the bumper stickers: "Driver under construction" or even better "Driver not of this world."

Then, my son, you will be a kipper.

As you repeat these steps over and over and over, the circle of bungee living will repeat. Feel the thrill and neglect your kids at the same time. That's Christian living.

The only thing that can break this cycle of bungee living is sin, because sin breaks the flow of God's power. Job's friends were right after all.

7

Making Jabez Mine, Mine, Mine

So God granted him what he requested.

I challenge you to make the Jabez mantra part of the daily grind of your meaningless, ordinary life. Follow the course outlined below for the next thirty days. By the end of that time, you'll notice that you will be able to despise ordinary life, suffocate your children, and be tempted by shallow things.

1. Chant the Jabez mantra every morning, and keep a record of your daily chants. Your words won't change, so just write "S.I." for "said it" on each day you S.I.

2. Write out the prayer, and tape it over everything material. This will help your eyes adjust to the coming transparency of things.

3. Reread this booklet once each week during the next month, then fall over and nap for a while, as your mind glazes over in exhaustion. Ask God to show you

important facts you may have missed. Once you realize that the four imperatives of this book are the same four that have showed up on evangelical bumper stickers for the past four decades, then you can stop reading the booklet and just stare at cars and repeat *paradigm shift, paradigm shift, paradigm shift.*

4. Tell another person—perhaps the postman or a grocery clerk—of your commitment to your mantra and ask them to check up on you, since the mantra makes you unable to check yourself.

5. Begin to keep a record of new opportunities for putting sentences into people's heads, but don't evaluate what you're saying; you're a Holy Spirit teacher now, and He can apparently say some goofy things.

6. Start praying the Jabez mantra for your family and friends, who will soon have a hard time remembering who you are since you've been so caught up in "real holy" work so much.

Of course, I have to say something now against the automaticity of the mantra. How about this? What you *know* about this mantra won't get you anything. Sure, you may say, What, huh? What about all those promises I made earlier. No, it's not your *knowledge*, but what you *believe* will happen next. Some sentences in your head are simply heavier than others.

THE REST OF THE STORY

After praying the mantra for thirty years like me, God will do mighty things through you.

I'm living proof.

I started praying the Jabez mantra way back in that yellow kitchen, with the rectangular drawers and AC electricity. Since that time, God has never stopped answering our prayers. We started teaching twenty Bible conferences a year. Our ministry will conduct over twenty-five hundred conferences a year, with ten magazines a month.

Now we want even more! We want to create a sentence-giver for every 50,000 people on earth! We want the whole world to turn God's faucet on and begin to hover above ground in the freshness of immaturity that will have absolutely no effect on material things! They will flee every temptation and think bumper stickers are profound literature and hate day-to-day life, and when that rapture thing happens no one will even notice they're missing! Now that's exhilaration! This is God's plan for earth! Unfortunately, I have to stop now, since I've used up my legal allotment of exclamation marks.

The Upturned Table Parody Series

The "upturned table" in our series name points back to Christ's anger with the merchants in the temple. Our parody series isn't as concerned with money in the Temple as it is with what modern Evangelicals spend on abject silliness. Now you can't say that sort of thing or publish parodies without someone pointing out that you're no genius yourself. And we don't claim to be. First, we see our parodies as sermons to ourselves before anyone else. For we too are responsible for the lame state of popular Evangelicalism today, even those of us who are from more classical Protestant backgrounds. We, too, exhibit some of the targets of our own barbs. Second, we also don't claim to sit aloof, all clean and wise, looking down on others' silliness. We are a part of the Evangelical community ourselves. These are our brothers who write these things; they represent us too. We have no doubts about their sincerity and good-hearted goals and wonderful characters, but we all must do light-years better.

The first response from many who love the books we aim to skewer is to be "wounded" and "offended," but that is the tiresome refuge of every little god who thinks blasphemy restrictions apply to him (oooh, notice the evil gender violation there). We all need to grow up and take the heat. But what about all those for whom these "precious" books have meant so much? One answer is that medieval folks could say the same thing about their relics. Relics made people feel warm and fuzzy too, but they were evidence of sickness.

Christian reality is a rich and fascinating blend of truth, beauty, and goodness. It is an exuberant love of life and light and celebration. Even with some of the glorious heights of Christian culture reached in prior eras, the Church still hasn't truly begun to plumb the magnificence of the Triune God. We're only scratching the surface, all the while non-Christian visions are perennially addicted to death. In order to mature, Evangelicals need to move beyond the bumper sticker shallowness of the past four decades and long for true wisdom. Parodying our silliness is one small nudge in that direction. *To whom much is given, much is expected.*

Be sure to visit the Canon Press web site:

www.canonpress.org
or call 1–800–488–2034

for such titles such as:

• *Angels in the Architecture: A Protestant Vision for Middle Earth* by Douglas Jones and Douglas Wilson (Canon Press)
• *Plowing in Hope: Toward a Biblical Theology of Culture* by David Bruce Hegeman (Canon Press)
• *Last Days Madness: Obsession of the Modern Church* by Gary DeMar (American Vision)
• *Postmillennialism: An Eschatology of Hope* by Keith A. Mathison (P & R Publ.)
• *A House for My Name: A Survey of the Old Testament* by Peter J. Leithart (Canon Press)
• *The Roar on the Other Side: A Guide for Student Poets* by Suzanne U. Clark (Canon Press)
• *Reforming Marriage* by Douglas Wilson (Canon Press)
• *Future Men: On Raising Boys* by Douglas Wilson (Canon Press)
. . . and more.

See *Credenda/Agenda* magazine too:
www.credenda.org